# Let's Take Care of the

MW00977937

The desert, the desert
is home to a snake.

# Let's take care of the desert.

The forest, the forest
is home to a bear.

Let's take care of the forest.

5

The ocean, the ocean
is home to a whale.

# Let's take care of the ocean.

The swamp, the swamp is home to an alligator.

8

# Let's take care of the swamp.

# The mountain, the mountain is home to a goat.

# Let's take care of the mountain.

The rain forest, the rain forest is home to a jaguar.

# Let's take care of the rain forest.

The desert,

the forest,

the ocean,

the swamp,

the mountain,

the rain forest.

15

The Earth, the Earth
is home to us all.
Let's take care of the Earth!